Withdrawn

CHEMISTS
IN ACTION

PUBLISHING COMPANY
WWW.CRABTREEBOOKS.COM

James Bow

Author: James Bow

Series research and development: Reagan Miller

Editorial director: Kathy Middleton

Photo research: James Nixon

Editors: Paul Humphrey, James Nixon, Ellen Rodger

Proofreader: Lorna Notsch

Designer: Keith Williams (sprout.uk.com)

Prepress technician: Samara Parent

Print coordinator: Katherine Berti

Layout: Keith Williams (sprout.uk.com)

Consultant: Brianne Manning

Produced for Crabtree Publishing Company
by Discovery Books

Cover image: A chemist wears protective gear while
analyzing a substance.

Photographs:

Alamy: pp. 4 (Mr Pics), 7 top (dpa picture alliance archive),
7 bottom (DOE Photo), 11 bottom (MediC Pix), 12 top
(Agencja Fotograficzna Caro), 14 bottom (Olaf Doering),
16 bottom (Jim West), 17 top (Universal Images Group
North America LLC), 26 (Science History Images).
Courtesy of Dr. Jamie Gallagher: p. 23.
Courtesy of Elif Bilgin: p. 27 top.
Flickr: p. 10 (Isabelle Saldana).
Getty Images: p. 25 bottom (BSIP/UIG).
NASA: pp. 19 top, 21 bottom (J. Rho/SSC/Caltech).
Shutterstock: pp. 5 top (Dmitry Kalinovsky), 5 bottom
(Nadezda Murmakova), 6 bottom (Motortion Films), 8
(Fejas), 9 middle (Humdan), 11 top (Ivan Chudakov),
12 bottom (Hanna Kuprevich), 14 top (Patrizio
Martorana), 15 (solarseven), 16 top (Microgen), 17 bottom
(Vshivkova), 18 top (Ditty_about_summer), 18 bottom
(vectorfusionart), 19 bottom (Gorodenkoff), 20 top
(Gorodenkoff), 20 bottom (Stefan Kunchev Kunchev), 21
middle (Dmitrijs Bindemanis), 22 top (ASDF_MEDIA), 22
bottom (Prath), 24 (FrameStockFootages), 25 top (Darren
Baker), 27 bottom (Antonov Roman), 28 top (Viktar
Malyshchyts), 28 bottom (Alexander Ruiz Acevedo).
Wikimedia: pp. 6 top (U.S. Department of Energy), 9 top, 9
bottom (Jonathunder), 13 (John Mainstone/University of
Queensland), 21 top (Justin15w).
All other images from Shutterstock

Library and Archives Canada Cataloguing in Publication

Bow, James, 1972-, author
        Chemists in action / James Bow.

(Scientists in action)
Includes index.
Issued in print and electronic formats.
ISBN 978-0-7787-5205-9 (hardcover).--
ISBN 978-0-7787-5216-5 (softcover).--
ISBN 978-1-4271-2157-8 (HTML)

        1. Chemists--Juvenile literature. 2. Chemistry--Juvenile literature.
I. Title.

QD35.B68 2018   j540   C2018-903001-1
                                                                      C2018-903002-X

Library of Congress Cataloging-in-Publication Data

Names: Bow, James, author.
Title: Chemists in action / James Bow.
Description: New York, New York : Crabtree Publishing, [2019] |
   Series: Scientists in action | Audience: Ages 10-14. | Audience:
   Grades 4 to 6. | Includes an index.
Identifiers: LCCN 2018033707 (print) | LCCN 2018034464 (ebook) |
   ISBN 9781427121578 (Electronic) |
   ISBN 9780778752059 (hardcover) |
   ISBN 9780778752165 (pbk.)
Subjects: LCSH: Chemistry--Juvenile literature. | Chemists--Juvenile
   literature.
Classification: LCC QD35 (ebook) | LCC QD35 .B69 2019 (print) |
   DDC 540--dc23
LC record available at https://lccn.loc.gov/2018033707

Crabtree Publishing Company
www.crabtreebooks.com   1-800-387-7650

Printed in the U.S.A./102018/CG20180810

Published in Canada
Crabtree Publishing
616 Welland Ave.
St. Catharines, Ontario
L2M 5V6

Published in the United States
Crabtree Publishing
PMB 59051
350 Fifth Avenue, 59th Floor
New York, New York 10118

Published in the United Kingdom
Crabtree Publishing
Maritime House
Basin Road North, Hove
BN41 1WR

Published in Australia
Crabtree Publishing
3 Charles Street
Coburg North
VIC, 3058

CONTENTS

THE SCIENCE OF MATTER

A bomb blast has rocked the neighborhood! Vehicles have been destroyed and windows are blown apart. Nobody got hurt, but there's so much damage, and so many questions. Who did this? What did they use? **Forensic** investigators arrive on the scene, but the place is a mess. Fortunately, the investigators have a secret weapon: They call chemists into action! Chemists have studied how explosives work. They know how to identify the smallest amounts of substances. They can find the evidence that shows how this blast occurred and who did it.

What Are Chemists?

Chemistry is the science of matter and its properties. Matter is any substance that takes up space and has mass. Properties describe the characteristics of matter; for example, is it a solid, a liquid, or a gas? Properties also include how certain types of matter interact with other types of matter, or how they interact with energy. Chemists study matter. They learn what different types of substances do, and how to work with these substances to make things happen, such as explosions.

Different chemicals burn with different-colored flames. Photographs of explosions can provide forensic chemists with clues about the types of bomb-making materials used.

Chemists in Action

In medicine, chemists research how substances react with the human body. They use this knowledge to create new drugs to cure illnesses. In forensics, chemists identify mystery substances, from poisons and bomb **residue** to blood, discovering evidence that solves crimes. In industry, chemists create materials, such as plastics, that are used to make new and better products. Chemists help the food industry find ways to make food last longer and taste better. Look around your home. Most things in there, from the plastic containers to the medicines in your bathroom, the paint on your walls, and even the best-before dates on your food are there because of chemists.

*A chemist researching new drugs wears a mask, hair net, and gloves so that she does not **contaminate** the substances she is studying.*

This book will follow chemists in many fields as they ask the questions that need to be answered. We will look at the problems they are still trying to solve. We will examine how chemists use science practices to guide their investigations and make discoveries.

Stronger than Steel

In the 1960s, American chemist Stephanie Kwolek was searching for a substitute for rubber, and instead found something that could stop a bullet! She was working with long, complex **molecules** called **polymers**, when the mixture didn't go right. It wasn't thick like rubber should be. Normally, she would have thrown it away. Instead, she ran it through a **spinneret**, and pulled out a long fiber. This fiber proved to be five times stronger than steel. Her company called it Kevlar. Woven into vests (left), Kevlar has saved the lives of thousands of police and military personnel. Sometimes, when scientists are looking to solve a question, they find answers to questions they weren't initially asking.

THE BIG QUESTIONS

Chemistry is at the heart of many other scientific fields. Chemists have a part to play in addressing some of the biggest questions of science.

One such question is: How did life begin on Earth? By studying fossils and simulating the conditions found on the early Earth, we know life started around 3.8 billion years ago. Scientists also think parts of Earth before then were covered in **primordial soup**. This was a combination of chemicals called **amino acids** found in the oceans. Amino acids are an important part of life, but they aren't alive. So what chemical processes happened to turn these amino acids into living things?

These chemists are developing technology that can generate fuels directly from sunlight.

Challenges for Today and Tomorrow

Another question is: How do we improve on **photosynthesis**? Most of our energy comes from the Sun; much of it stored in the leaves of plants millions of years ago and buried underground where they became **fossil fuels** like oil and coal. If we could capture and store the Sun's energy as easily as plants do it, we could solve Earth's energy crisis!

In medicine, chemists are looking for the perfect drug, or set of drugs, that can cure all illnesses without side effects. Many physical and mental health problems have chemical causes, but the body is complicated, and finding the right medicine takes a lot of research.

Medicines are chemicals that interact with your body.

Modern life would not be possible without chemistry. Chemists have invented many materials that have made our lives easier, from cheaper fabrics for clothes to disposable diapers, plastic packaging, and more. Unfortunately, this comes at the cost of a lot of garbage that doesn't break down. To save us from being buried under our own waste, and to save us from running out of materials, chemists are hunting for new materials that can be easily **recycled** or are **biodegradable**.

*These chemists have invented a biodegradable foil using **proteins** from peas.*

The Branches of Chemistry

Chemistry is a wide field, and chemists will specialize or work in one of a number of branches. Organic chemistry is the study of substances containing carbon. Carbon is a molecule that makes up living tissue. Biochemistry is a part of organic chemistry that focuses on the chemical processes that take place inside living things. Inorganic chemistry is the chemistry of metals and gases. Physical chemistry studies how matter and energy interact, such as how things change or explode when you apply heat. You will find chemists working in many different industries, from scientific research to energy production, to inventing and testing new materials, to protecting the environment.

This chemist is testing a new material to be used in batteries.

A CHANGING PROFESSION

Chemistry was one of the first tools of civilization. More than 7,000 years ago, ancient peoples in southeastern Europe used fire and other tools to melt metals such as tin, lead, and copper out of stones, or **ores**. They made these metals into tools, weapons, and jewelry. Mixing metals changed their properties. Harder steel was invented in China around 250 BCE, when metalworkers mixed charcoal with iron.

In Europe, around the 1100s, early chemists, known as alchemists, looked for the "spirit of the universe" in substances. They believed metals were alive and grew inside Earth. Alchemists mixed these substances, believing, for example, they could turn lead into gold. Despite such incorrect theories, alchemists wrote down their observations, building our understanding of substances and how they work.

Finding the Elements

Alchemy became chemistry when Paracelsus (1493–1541) rejected the age-old idea that everything was made of a combination of earth, air, fire, and water. Chemists realized that different substances were made of different **atoms** and molecules. In 1778, Frenchman Antoine Lavoisier noted that air wasn't just one thing. He identified the gas oxygen and discovered how important it was in **combustion**. With this understanding, new and more powerful tools were made, including explosives, such as gunpowder.

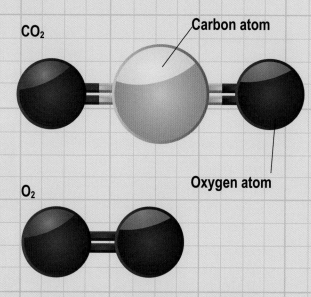

Air is a mixture of many gases, including oxygen and **carbon dioxide**. A carbon dioxide molecule (CO_2) is one carbon atom joined to two oxygen atoms. An oxygen molecule (O_2) consists of two oxygen atoms.

By the 1800s, chemists knew there were at least 66 different types of atoms, which they called **elements**. Russian chemist Dmitri Mendeleev (right) looked at the properties of these elements and arranged them on a **periodic table**, based on their differences in weight. This chart had gaps in it that he realized would be filled in by elements not yet discovered. Today, we know there are 92 elements in nature, from the lightest, hydrogen, to the heaviest, uranium. Chemists have created another 26.

The Mother of Other Sciences

Starting in the late 1800s, other science fields branched off from chemistry. Physicists looked closer at the natural forces that made atoms work, while chemists continued to look at how atoms and molecules interacted with each other. Some chemists developed new materials like plastic and Kevlar. Organic chemists developed biochemistry, exploring how chemical reactions inside living things help keep organisms alive.

Chemists are learning new things every day, inventing new materials, and gaining a better understand of the reasons how things react with each other. Chemistry continues to help many different fields answer important questions.

Nobel Prize winners receive a gold medallion showing the face of Alfred Nobel.

All known elements in the universe are listed in the periodic table, including the gases hydrogen and oxygen.

Alfred Nobel

The Nobel Prize was founded by the Swedish chemist Alfred Nobel in 1901. Early in his life, he invented many explosives, including dynamite. He'd done this to help in mining. It made him rich. Unfortunately, he lost his brother to an explosives accident, and saw dynamite used as a weapon in war. On his death, he gave his fortune to set up prizes for works creating "the greatest benefit on mankind" in chemistry, physics, medicine, literature, and peace.

SCIENTIFIC INVESTIGATION

Chemists, like all scientists, ask questions about the world around them. They follow science practices (see box) as they investigate. Although practices can vary in different branches, all scientists use at least some of these practices. They repeat some or all of the steps as needed, as they search for evidence and reach conclusions.

Science Practices

- Asking questions
- Developing methods of investigation, including building **models** and designing observations and experiments
- Carrying out investigations
- Analyzing and interpreting data collected
- Using mathematics and technology to process data
- Constructing explanations from evidence
- Communicating findings and conclusions

Steps in Science

Some scientists plan and carry out experiments to find their answers. Others build models to explore their theories. They then interpret and analyze the data that they get from their experiments or models. Sometimes, scientists use computers and mathematics to help explain what they've found. They then discuss the evidence they've gathered, communicating their information and conclusions to other scientists.

A chemist observes a chemical reaction during an experiment.

Investigating in the field is challenging, but like other scientists, chemists have to go to where the data can be found.

Not every scientist investigates by conducting experiments in a laboratory. Forensic chemists, for example, visit crime scenes, using observation to gather evidence and information out in the **field**. A biochemist studying how pollution is affecting trees in a forest has to go to the forest to see what is happening. Field scientists use tools and instruments such as **spectrometers** to test samples and to collect and record data.

From the Field: Christopher Barrett

Canadian materials chemist Christopher Barrett leads a team at McGill University in Montréal, investigating the ways that complex molecules, such as polymers, can change their shape in the presence of a trigger, such as electricity or light. Materials science is a branch of chemistry in which scientists try to invent new substances. One of the goals of materials science is to make substances that react to triggers to perform certain tasks. This way, a material could behave like a machine, but it would be a single substance, rather than a bunch of parts that can break down or fall apart. Barrett and his team are conducting experiments in the lab. Their data are being analyzed, and the findings will be shared in a number of **scientific journals**.

A chemist uses a spectrometer to learn about molecules that are found in the brain.

11

THE POWERS OF OBSERVATION

Chemists, like other scientists, use observation as they try to understand how substances work, or how they interact with the environment. They often observe chemical reactions in the laboratory to find answers to the questions they are asking. Chemists studying the environment can test samples of water from lakes and streams to identify **pollutants**. Forensic chemists collect samples at crime scenes and use chemistry to determine if, for example, a fiber is a hair or a piece of fabric. They can detect residues of explosives or poisons. Every observation is a clue that could solve a mystery.

Even in the field, forensic chemists dress to ensure they do not contaminate potential evidence.

Measure by Measure

Chemists identify substances by carefully measuring their characteristics. How much does a certain amount of a substance weigh? At what temperature does it freeze, melt, or become a gas? How does it react with other substances, such as oxygen, water, or acids? Measurements need to be precise, which is why a lot of chemistry takes place in the laboratory. Chemists need **controlled conditions** to test their samples, so that things they didn't plan for don't mess up or contaminate their results.

Pasteur pipettes, also known as eye droppers, allow chemists to transfer small quantities of chemicals without exposing them to the environment.

Sometimes observation uncovers unexpected results. In 2009, a chemist at Oregon State University discovered a new color. He just happened to be mixing different elements and chemicals in a furnace, and when the mixture came out, it was a bright shade of blue. Fortunately, the student wrote down what he had done, and other scientists were able to repeat the test. The new **pigment** is already being used in crayons!

The Pitch Drop Experiment

Experiments can take a while. In 1927, Professor Thomas Parnell wanted to demonstrate that some things we think of as solid are actually very **viscous** liquids. Observing these slow liquids could teach us how faster fluids behave. He heated pitch, a black, sticky substance made from wood tar, poured it into a funnel, let it cool, then cut the bottom out of the funnel to let the pitch flow.

The droplets of pitch form and fall about once a decade. When Parnell retired, he gave control of the experiment to Professor John Mainstone. Neither he nor Mainstone were present when the first droplet of pitch finally separated and fell. Attempts to capture the pitch drop on camera failed, as the moment was too unpredictable.

Professor Mainstone died in 2013, before the ninth drop of pitch fell. Professor Andrew White now handles what is currently the world's longest ongoing laboratory experiment. There is enough pitch to keep the experiment going for another 100 years!

Professor John Mainstone in 1990, two years after the seventh drop of pitch fell.

ASKING THE QUESTIONS

Chemists ask questions about matter. They explore what substances are and what they do, and how they react and change if energy or other substances are added. For some chemists, the search for answers is a hunt for suspects. What sort of hazardous waste was dumped into the environment, and who put it there? What factories are the sources of air pollution?

Hunting Down the Clues

For a forensic chemist arriving at a bomb site, he or she knows that explosions are just violent chemical reactions. Substances were mixed together with energy, which changed the substances and released greater amounts of energy. So, what were the substances? How were they mixed together?

An environmental chemist gathers water samples to identify pollution at a site.

In medicine, testing many samples shows chemists how drugs react under different conditions.

Chemists working in medicine ask similar questions. How will a new substance react with living tissue? Will it be poisonous? Can it be used as a medicine? What side effects will it cause? How much of the substance can people take before they are harmed? Physical chemists explore which substances cause the biggest reactions, which helps them develop more effective explosives or better sources of energy.

From the Field: Ben Clifton

Australian biochemist Ben Clifton is searching for the answers on how the chemistry of the early Earth created life. Scientific theories about the early Earth suggest that the planet was covered in complex molecules such as amino acids. There was heat and lightning, adding energy for all sorts of chemical reactions. But how did this mixture create life?

Clifton is looking at modern **enzymes**. These are special molecules that are important to life because they speed up the chemical reactions in our bodies that we depend on to live. By comparing the differences between modern enzymes and their ancestors, Clifton is seeing how today's enzymes evolved over time, and identifying what enzymes were like during the early Earth. Understanding how enzymes change over time not only helps scientists understand how life formed on Earth, it also can help chemists take this evolution forward, by changing enzymes to help make new medicines.

During the early days of Earth, comets and meteors may have brought water and other chemicals responsible for the creation of life on our planet.

The Never-ending Search

The search for answers doesn't stop once the answers are found. Research and investigation often create more questions that require further research and investigation. For example, in 1928, chemists discovered chlorofluorocarbons (CFCs). These molecules didn't catch fire, so they were soon used to safely help air conditioners cool and make aerosol cans work. However, chemist Mario Molina wondered what happened to CFCs after they were released into the atmosphere. His investigation showed that CFCs were harming the environment by destroying Earth's **ozone layer**. Today, CFCs are banned worldwide.

CHEMISTS ON THE CASE!

Now that a team of chemists has a question, how do they find the answer? They don't just guess. They follow a careful plan, or **methodology**, in order to gather data and evidence. This is not only a plan for how to conduct their experiment, it also shows other scientists what was done, so they can conduct their own experiments and confirm whether the initial results were accurate.

Searching for samples of fabric or residue can be like finding a microscopic needle in a haystack, but forensic chemists are up to the challenge.

Chemical Fingerprints

At a bomb site, the forensic chemist takes samples from the rubble in an attempt to find out what caused the explosion. He or she observes and measures everything possible. The size and shape of the blast hint that particular bomb materials were used. Different bombs also leave behind different residues. In the laboratory, data from these samples are entered into computers and compared to identify these residues. Forensic chemistry is even used at ancient sites. Chemical analysis of **mummies** from ancient Egypt tell us a lot about how people lived, what foods they ate, and how they made the mummies in the first place.

Environmental chemists look for similar clues to identify the sources of pollution in waterways, on land, or in the air. Chemists working in agriculture take soil samples and test their **pH** to see whether the soil is acidic or not, and how many nutrients the soil has. This helps farmers figure out what crops can grow and what **fertilizers** are needed.

Some forensic chemists work to analyze and identify old bones.

A Simulated Search

Biochemists testing new drugs go through many investigations to make sure their drugs are safe and work the way they're supposed to. Before biochemists can try these drugs on human volunteers, they have to test them on animals like rats and monkeys. However, animal testing is controversial. Scientists are working on computer programs that can simulate how human **cells** react to different substances. This way, biochemists can test new drugs without putting animal or human lives at risk.

Three-dimensional (3-D) glasses and computer programs help chemists observe molecular models.

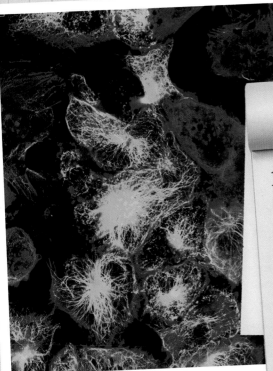

Cancer cells glow under a microscope.

From the Field: Marina Tanasova and Smitha Rao

One of the keys to surviving cancer is finding it early. Michigan Tech researchers Marina Tanasova (a chemist) and Smitha Rao (a biomedical engineer) wondered if they could find a quicker way to detect cancer. They knew all cells need sugar to live, and they knew cancer cells take in a certain type of sugar at a faster rate. So, what if they created a special sugar molecule that glowed under certain lights? By adding this sugar to a patient's bloodstream, cancer cells could absorb these molecules and be detected by their glow. Tanasova and Rao are currently testing different types of sugar molecules to see which work best.

TOOLS OF THE TRADE

When you think of chemists, you may think of a person in a white lab coat pouring substances into beakers and heating them on a Bunsen burner. A lot of chemists do fit this description, but there are other tools chemists use in their experiments.

For example, chemists often use spectrometers to identify mystery substances. A spectrometer shines light at a substance and measures the light that's reflected back. Each substance reflects light differently, producing a unique pattern of colors. Some spectrometers use different types of light or radiation. X-ray and nuclear MRI spectrometers, for example, can be used to look inside things, or under things, and identify things beneath the surface.

Microscopes are one of the most important tools for a chemist.

Looking Closer

Tools like **electron microscopes** help chemists look really closely at substances, allowing them to see the very atoms and molecules they are made of. **Centrifuges** separate chemicals by spinning them around. Heavier elements are pulled farther out by the force of the spin. Chemists can explore the characteristics of a chemical, adding heat energy to find the melting point and boiling point.

An important part of chemistry is precision. To identify the substances they are working with, or to build new materials, everything must be carefully measured. Very accurate scales weigh substances. Precise thermometers measure how hot things are. The metric system is used by every scientist to record results, ensuring that scientists around the world can share, compare, and understand the data.

Centrifuges can pull out substances that are dissolved in liquids.

Using satellites, scientists have already discovered evidence of water vapor on a planet trillions of miles from Earth.

New Technologies

As technology has advanced, chemists have developed new tools to conduct their experiments. Computers keep track of and analyze complex data. Computer simulations can model dangerous chemical reactions without putting lab workers at risk. Lasers allow scientists to measure things even more precisely than before. Microfluidic chips are slides etched with very small channels designed to test for and experiment on minute amounts of certain substances—it is like having a chemistry lab in the palm of your hand. Satellites high above Earth can identify chemicals from a great distance. They can track pollution back on the ground, or even chemicals on other planets, showing the presence of water, or even possibly life.

Keep It Safe

Substances can be **toxic**, or can react violently with other substances and explode. Chemists must prepare themselves and their lab to stay safe. Ventilation hoods are placed above laboratory workspaces to suck away any toxic gases that may form during an experiment. Chemists test small amounts of substances and use safety goggles, gloves, and sometimes blast shields to protect themselves from violent reactions. If they need lots of protection, they wear hazmat suits that cover the whole body, and masks to keep the air they breathe safe.

Hazmat suits come with their own air supply to make sure chemists don't breathe dangerous toxic gases.

CONCLUSIONS FROM DATA

Once chemists gather data from the field, they come back to the laboratory and analyze the information. They make maps, models, charts, tables, and other visual aids that help them interpret their findings. Then they make conclusions that are supported by the evidence that they have gathered.

Computers help scientists organize data, which makes it easier to interpret the results.

A forensic chemist studying samples from a bomb site may find residue of a particular type of explosive made from fertilizer. The evidence might show that a vehicle packed with this material had caused the explosion. The conclusions made by chemists help investigators catch criminals and terrorists and bring them to justice.

Following the Evidence, No Matter Where It Takes You

Chemists follow the evidence carefully and will come to conclusions that range from disturbing to inspiring. In 1896, Swedish chemist Svante Arrhenius discovered that carbon dioxide gas traps more heat in the atmosphere, causing a **greenhouse effect**. Scientists measuring carbon dioxide levels now realize that they are higher than they have been in the past 800,000 years. This is causing our planet to heat up, changing our climate.

Factories have contributed to the rise in levels of carbon dioxide.

In the 1960s, biochemists at the Research Triangle Institute in North Carolina discovered that a chemical found in the bark of the Pacific yew tree could be used to make medicines that destroy cancer cells. However, the yew tree is hard to grow, and it takes years before the drug can be harvested. Investigating this molecule, other biochemists at Florida State University were able to successfully **synthesize** the chemical in the lab. This means they can make this cancer-fighting chemical without having to grow more trees.

Similarly, materials scientists looking for ways to reduce the amount of trash in the world recently discovered that combining the material from shrimp shells with spider silk proteins creates a hard, tough plastic that is still biodegradable. These types of conclusions give chemists, and everyone, hope for a better world.

The Pacific yew only grows on the West Coast of North America.

Getting spiders to make enough spider silk is a challenge, which is why chemists are trying to create the substance in the lab.

From the Field: Olivia Harper Wilkins

How do you measure the chemistry of stars? Olivia Harper Wilkins is an **astrochemist**. Using extremely powerful telescopes and spectrometers, she has identified nearly 200 different types of molecules in the interstellar medium. The interstellar medium is the space between **solar systems** in the galaxy. Among these molecules is glycolaldehyde, which is a key part of **RNA**, a molecule that is an important ingredient in the formation of life. This may be one of the best pieces of evidence yet that life has a chance of forming on other worlds.

SHARING THE CHEMISTRY

Like all scientists, once chemists have gone through their investigations and arrived at their conclusions, they report on what they've found. By telling other scientists and the public what they have learned through their observations and experiments, they teach us more about the world we live in. They also help find solutions to problems we're facing, such as pollution. by discovering new materials or new sources of energy, chemists make our lives easier and show how to reduce our impact on the environment.

A chemist displays her findings to other scientists.

The Science Report

Chemists write reports about their findings. These explain the questions they asked and their methodology. A report shows how they gathered their data, what the data showed, and how the evidence points to the conclusions they reached.

Chemists, like other scientists, use maps, graphs, tables, and pictures to show the data they discovered. For example, a forensic chemist who discovered a bomb residue may be called to court to show how he or she discovered that evidence, and how the terrorists built their bomb and used it. An environmental chemist hunting down sources of pollution may use maps and charts as part of a presentation to show that pollution levels are highest around nearby factories.

Forensic evidence must be protected from future contamination, so that it can be tested again, if necessary.

A Wider Audience

Chemists share their findings with as wide an audience as possible. Their reports may be printed in books, newspapers, or special magazines called scientific journals that focus on the latest scientific discoveries. They often gather online or at conferences to give speeches and post videos explaining their research. Chemists share their knowledge, find new questions to investigate, and look for better ways to research and pursue investigations.

Dr. Jamie Gallagher pleases the crowd with a fiery chemistry demonstration.

From the Field: Jamie Gallagher

Jamie Gallagher is a Scottish chemist and materials scientist who spends his time sharing his passion for science. Since 2009, he has been giving live shows, combining comedy, explosive scientific demonstrations, and dance, to thousands of people each year. He has also appeared on television and radio programs around the world. His shows demonstrate the wonders of chemistry, including the discovery of new materials and energy sources, while highlighting the challenges future scientists face, such as dealing with the problems of plastic in the environment. His goal is to get as many people as possible passionate about science, so they can become the scientists of the future to meet these challenges.

TEAM SCIENCE!

An important part of science is **collaboration**. Chemists share their work so that other scientists can learn from it and build on that knowledge. This helps the scientific community as a whole understand complex problems. By working together, scientists bring different skills, different tools, and new ways of looking at old problems.

Collaboration aids creativity, allowing scientists to generate new ideas, new questions, and new answers.

Peer Review

Peer review is an important part of scientific investigation. Chemists can't just accept each other's conclusions without testing them. Chemists share their work so that other scientists can review the methodology, test the data, and make sure the conclusions are supported by the evidence.

Scientific journals publish the research of chemists and other scientists. This allows other scientists from the field to examine and test the work. Scientists search for errors that may have occurred while collecting the data, or mistakes that may have been made when analyzing the data. They make sure there aren't any flaws in the logic or **bias** in the research.

Chemists repeat investigations made by other scientists to check their findings.

Avoiding Bias

Bias happens when a scientist influences the results of a study. This might be intentional: For example, a chemist working for a company might be asked to downplay findings showing that one of its factories has released pollutants into a nearby lake. However, most of the time, a scientist doesn't realize he or she is adding personal bias to an experiment. When testing drugs that fight diseases, it's natural for chemists to want the drug to work. Every scientist's peers must test the findings of every experiment to ensure that conclusions are accurate, and the science can be trusted.

The American Chemical Society

With more than 150,000 members in 140 countries, the American Chemical Society (acs.org) is the largest scientific society in the world. Founded in 1876, the organization publishes scientific journals and runs conferences at which chemists and representatives from different industries, universities, and governments can meet and share knowledge. The ACS promotes the teaching of chemistry in schools, encourages children to take an interest in chemistry, and helps people looking to advance in a chemistry career. It also offers a standard for all chemists to live up to, promoting the advancement of scientific knowledge without bias, as well as safety in the chemistry lab.

The organization also keeps a catalogue of different chemical substances identified or invented by its members. It currently has registered more than 130 million!

A chemist demonstrates the properties and makeup of medicines, such as aspirin, at a kids' workshop.

THE FUTURE OF CHEMISTRY

Chemistry has changed the world. Chemists created plastics that are in many of the products we use every day, and the pollution that comes with these products. Chemists have produced some of the most important drugs in medicine, and some illegal drugs as well.

The way forward will see chemists both address the challenges that have been created and explore new ways to improve our lives. New drugs and medicines could cure cancers. New fuels could help us reduce pollution and fight climate change. Materials scientists are experimenting with new materials like carbon **nanotubes** and spider silk that are stronger and lighter than Kevlar. Forensic chemists are looking at new ways to detect explosives to prevent terrorist attacks. They are also exploring new ways to detect hidden evidence, making it even easier for police to catch criminals.

Chemists are needed in many fields, from environmental protection to law enforcement to industry. They will be asked to solve the challenges of tomorrow, from building new materials to cleaning up waste and finding new sources of energy. They'll even be needed to solve chemical mysteries among the stars. As long as there are questions for chemists to answer, the need for chemists will only grow.

Carbon nanotubes are grown by getting carbon atoms to arrange themselves into long, tubelike molecules.

Get Started Now!

If chemistry interests you, you don't have to wait to get through school before doing some investigations yourself. Elif Bilgin, a 16-year-old student in Istanbul, Turkey, was worried about pollution in her city, a lot of it caused by plastic, which is made out of oil. She asked if plastic could be made out of something else that wouldn't damage the environment so much. She looked at discarded banana peels and investigated ways these could be turned into plastic. She worked for more than two years, but finally she found a solution that made a plastic that had all the characteristics she wanted. She received a $50,000 prize from the Google Science Fair and is looking to improve her formula for the growing **bioplastics** industry.

Elif Bilgin works on her banana investigation in her kitchen.

You, too, can be a chemist in action! Start an investigation on the environment around your home.

Chemistry at Home

Chemistry is everywhere, so why not run an investigation yourself? Chemists sometimes test the condition of water and soil. You could try collecting your own samples. Not only can you learn more about chemistry, you'll also find answers you didn't know before about your own neighborhood. Turn the page to start your own investigation.

INVESTIGATE!

The first step of any investigation is asking a question. For example, how acidic is the soil in your garden? How do we test for this? What can we do to make soil less acidic? Write down your questions and gather materials from this list:

Materials

- A small red cabbage
- Pot of boiling water
- Strainer
- Two large bowls or pots
- A grater
- Measuring spoons
- Clear glass or plastic containers to observe reactions
- Masking tape and markers to label things
- Lemon juice
- Vinegar
- Baking soda

Red cabbage contains a chemical called anthocyanin, which is naturally purple, but changes color in an acid or a **base** environment.

Procedure:

1 First, you can make an **indicator** that will tell us whether a sample is acidic or a base. Take your red cabbage and grate about half of it. Put the grated cabbage in a large bowl or pot.

2 Boil some water. Once it's boiling, pour it over the cabbage. The cabbage should just be covered.

3 Let the cabbage sit in the water, stirring it occasionally, until the water is at room temperature. This will take at least an hour.

4 Pour the cabbage water through a strainer into another large bowl or pot. Squeeze or shake the cabbage to get as much color into the water as you can. The result should be a bowl full of blue or purple liquid. This is your indicator. You can discard the cabbage.

5 It's time to test your indicator to make sure it's working. You'll need two cups for the test. Add 1 tablespoon (15 ml) of indicator to each.

6 Use something we know is an acid, such as lemon juice or vinegar, and something we know is a base, such as baking soda. Put a few drops of acid into one cup of indicator and a sprinkle of baking soda into the other cup of indicator. Gently swirl them to mix. If the indicator is working, it should change color. Pink or red indicates an acid. Green or yellow indicates a base. Things that are neither an acid or a base, like distilled water, should not change the color of the indicator.

7 Now that you know your indicator is working, you're ready to conduct some chemistry in the field. Gather soil samples from around your neighborhood. Envelopes or labeled jars are both good collection tools. Be sure to write down where each sample came from. In the same way as in step six, test soil samples to see if they are acidic or basic. Write down your observations.

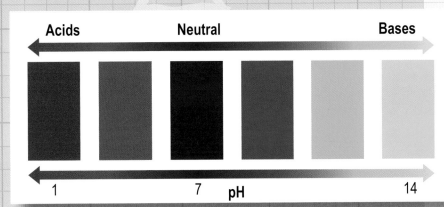

Analyze Your Data!

Once you have finished your observations, be sure to write down your findings. Use charts to help show what you've discovered — you might, for example, put colors on a map. Were soils from different locations more or less acidic than in other locations? Can you think of reasons why? Pollution from road traffic may have an effect, for example. Be sure to communicate the results of your findings and tell others to conduct their own experiments, too. That way, we can all be like scientists, answering questions about the world around us.

This pH color chart for a red cabbage juice indicator will tell you how acidic or not your sample is.

LEARNING MORE

BOOKS

Coelho, Alexa, and Simon Field. *Why Is Milk White?: & 200 Other Curious Chemistry Questions.* Chicago Review Press, 2013.

Connolly, Sean. *Book of Disturbingly Dangerous Chemistry.* Workman Publishing, 2018.

Gray, Theodore W., and Nick Mann. *Molecules: The Elements and the Architecture of Everything.* Black Dog & Leventhal Publishers, 2018.

Loh-Hagan, Virginia. *The Real Marie Curie.* Cherry Lake Publishing, 2018.

Losure, Mary. *Isaac the Alchemist.* Candlewick Press, 2018. (A narrative nonfiction book about Sir Isaac Newton as a child, learning about science through alchemy.)

Martin, Claudia. *Materials.* Capstone Press Inc., 2018.

Wood, Alix. *Backyard Chemistry Experiments.* Powerkids Press, 2018.

ONLINE

http://mocomi.com/learn/science/chemistry/
Learn about chemistry through fun activities, including interactive media articles, videos, and fun projects.

www.acs.org/content/acs/en/education/whatischemistry/adventures-in-chemistry.html
Enjoy learning about chemistry with these fun experiments and games.

www.chem4kids.com
Learn all about the elements of chemistry with informative articles and quizzes.

www.sciencekids.co.nz/chemistry.html
Discover the world of chemistry through experiments you can do at home, as well as games, lessons, and facts.

https://education.jlab.org
Offering many science resources for students and teachers alike, including games, puzzles, videos, and links to events.

www.strangematterexhibit.com
A website about materials science and how things are made.

GLOSSARY

amino acid A chemical substance made from organic molecules that make up a large portion of living things, such as our cells

astrochemist A scientist who studies the chemistry of outer space

atom The smallest unit of an element, molecules are made from atoms

base A substance that reacts with acid and makes it less acidic

bias To believe something is true in spite of evidence that shows it's not, or to allow something to change the results so that they aren't true

biodegradable Describes something that is able to break down and decay over time

bioplastics Type of plastics that are made from plants rather than from oil

carbon dioxide A colorless gas that animals breathe out, is used by plants in photosynthesis, and is produced when a fuel containing carbon is burned

cell The smallest piece of a living thing that grows and helps the living thing to live

centrifuge A machine that spins to separate liquids of different densities

collaboration When people work together toward a common goal

combustion When something catches on fire and burns

contaminate When something is added to a substance that changes it or makes it impure

controlled conditions An experiment in which unexpected changes or influences are kept out

electron microscope A microscope that uses a beam of electrons in order to see really small objects, like atoms

element A substance that is made entirely of one type of atom

enzyme A substance produced by living organisms that makes certain chemical reactions happen

fertilizer Special chemicals that feed plants and help them grow

field The natural environment, rather than a laboratory

forensic Describes scientific methods of investigating crime

fossil fuel Fuel such as oil, coal, and natural gas made from remains of plants and animals that died millions of years ago

greenhouse effect When certain gases in the atmosphere, such as carbon dioxide, trap the Sun's heat and keep Earth warm

indicator A substance that changes its appearance in the presence of a different substance

methodology A set of instructions or records showing how an experiment or other task was done

model An object or image used to show or explain an idea

molecule The smallest particle of a substance, made from two or more atoms

mummies Dead bodies that have been wrapped in cloths dipped in preserving chemicals

nanotube A tube-shaped molecule made of a special arrangement of atoms

ore A type of rock containing metals or other valuable substances

ozone layer A part of the atmosphere containing higher than normal amounts of the gas ozone, which blocks dangerous ultraviolet radiation from the Sun

peer review A process during which other scientists review a scientist's work and test it to make sure it's true

periodic table A chart of the different elements, arranged by their weight and other characteristics

pH A measurement of how acidic or how much of a base a substance is; an acronym for "power of hydrogen"; extremely acidic substances have a pH of 0, where as extremely basic substances have a pH of 14. Distilled water is neutral, or 7

photosynthesis A process in which plants take the Sun's energy, water, and carbon dioxide and change them into sugar and oxygen

pigment A chemical substance used to color things, such as paints

pollutant A substance that is harmful to the environment

polymer A substance made up of long chains of molecules

primordial soup A substance rich in organic molecules

protein A long molecule made of organic chemicals, including amino acids, that helps build things like body tissue and hair

recycle To take something and use it as raw material to make another thing

residue A small trace of something that is left behind

RNA Stands for ribonucleic acid; a molecule used by living organisms to carry instructions on how to build their cells

scientific journal A magazine or other publication where scientific research is published

solar system A system in which planets revolve around a star, such as the Sun in our solar system

spectrometer A machine that uses reflected laser light to identify different chemicals or substances

spinneret A machine that produces long fibers out of a liquid

synthesize To make a copy of something that exists in nature

toxic Describes something harmful to living things

viscous Describes a liquid that is thick and slow moving

INDEX

ABOUT THE AUTHOR

James Bow is the author of more than 50 nonfiction books for children. He is a graduate with a bachelor's degree in environmental science. He tries to make sure that the science experiments in his two daughters' rooms don't get out of hand.